Paul's Letter to the Colossians

George Stevens, Douglas Pettman,
Ernie Brown, George Bell, Gordon Kell
and David Anderson

Edited by John D Rice

Scripture Truth Publications

PAUL'S LETTER TO THE COLOSSIANS

This book is based on material previously broadcast in the "Truth for Today" progamme on London's Premier Radio in June and July 2000.
Copyright © 2000 Truth for Today

First published August 2016
Typeset and transferred to Digital Printing 2016
ISBN: 978-0-901860-95-8 (paperback)
Copyright © 2016 John D Rice and Scripture Truth Publications

Cover photograph: Ancient City Laodikeia, Denizli, Turkey © tolgatezcan / Fotolia

Published by Scripture Truth Publications
31-33 Glover Street, Crewe, Cheshire, CW1 3LD

Scripture Truth is an imprint of Central Bible Hammond Trust, a charitable trust

Typesetting by John Rice
Printed and bound by Lightning Source

Foreword

When considering suitable Bible Study material for young Christians on the subject of Paul's letter to the believers at Colossae, my thoughts turned to the series of talks on the letter given by different speakers on the *Truth for Today* radio programme in 2000. No constraints were placed on the structure of these talks: some speakers took a verse-by-verse approach to their allotted passage of the book, others a more thematic approach. In bringing this collection together, the individual approaches have been retained, with the introduction of subheadings, to enable the book to be used for both devotional and study purposes. Scripture quotations have been standardised on one translation, to provide a consistent approach to the text.

As you read, allow the Holy Spirit to work out in your life the faith, love and hope, so evident in the church at Colossae, in response to the letter's glorious theme that *Christ is everything!*

John Rice

July 2016

PAUL'S LETTER TO THE COLOSSIANS

Contents

PAUL'S LETTER TO THE COLOSSIANS

Introduction

BY GEORGE STEVENS

In the days of the Apostle Paul, Colossae was merely a small town which was part of the Roman province of Asia. It is likely that the Gospel reached the town while Paul was living in Ephesus (Acts 19:10). However, it seems that Paul may never have visited the town himself, but one of his fellow Christians, Epaphras, is thought to have carried the good news of Christ to the area. In fact, it was Epaphras who brought a report of the church to the Apostle, which prompted this letter from prison.

The letter shows us how Paul deals with the false teachings which were permeating the church.

- An important place was given by the false teachers to the powers of the spirit world. This degraded the Person and work of Christ.

  Paul combats this by teaching that Christ is the One in whom the fullness of the Godhead dwells, even the Creator and Lord of all things in heaven and in earth.

- Outward observances such as feasts, fasts, new moons, Sabbaths and circumcision were wrongly emphasized, along with a form of works to gain righteousness.

Paul argues that it is through the work of Christ that we have peace with God and, furthermore, that we, as a result, should "put on" Christ (3:10-12). That is to say, to live lives in the power of the Spirit which reveal the life of Christ in and through us.

- A philosophy of "higher" wisdom, knowledge and understanding was prevalent.

  Paul resists this by showing that the revealed secret of God (the "mystery") is found in Christ alone (1:27).

Therefore, in overall terms, we may say that the letter deals with the glories of Christ as Head over all things to the Church.

The letter may be broadly split into three main sections:

1. an *introduction* marked by thanksgivings and prayer for the Colossian believers (1:1-14);

2. a *doctrinal section* which deals with the supremacy of Christ viewed from every aspect (1:15 to 2:3); and,

3. a *practical section* warning against error, noting the results of union with Christ and giving final greetings to the Colossians (2:4 to 4:18).

Colossians 1:1-18
Pre-eminence in all things

BY GEORGE STEVENS

This first section of the letter concludes with the pre-eminence of Christ in all things. The eighteen verses may be divided as follows:

- Verses 1-2: Paul's greetings;

- Verses 3-6: Paul's gratitude for their faith, love, hope and fruitfulness;

- Verses 7-8: Paul's appreciation of Epaphras;

- Verses 9-11: Paul's intercession for their spiritual growth;

- Verses 12-13: The Father's work;

- Verses 14-18: The glories of Christ in relation to God, creation, the Church and all things.

COLOSSIANS 1:1-2 — PAUL'S GREETINGS

Paul begins his greetings by expressing his Apostleship. He was not just a 'sent one', which is the meaning of the word 'apostle', but one who had been directly commissioned and sent by the risen and exalted Christ Jesus. This

9

commission was by 'divine will'. That meant, Paul had the God-given authority to represent the anointed Saviour.

Timothy is identified with Paul in the writing of this letter. Paul calls him, literally, "the brother" (verse 1, N.Tr.). In this way he emphasizes the universal relationship between Christians as members of a family. The use of the definite article seems to show that Timothy is a good model of what every Christian brother should be like. Of course, Timothy, whose name means "honoured of God", is called a man of God. This should always be our aim as children of God, whether male or female.

Paul writes "to the *saints* and faithful *brethren* in Christ who are in Colossae." The two nouns apply to the members of the same company. A 'saint', in the context of the New Testament, is simply a believer in the Lord Jesus Christ seen from God's point of view. The word means 'holy' or 'set apart'. Every Christian is classed as a saint. Each one is set apart for the possession, pleasure and purposes of God. If this is true *positionally* then, by the power of the Spirit of God, it should be worked out *practically* in our lives. They should be God-steered, holy lives. These Christians are also called "*faithful* brethren". Not only were they all related to one another in Christ, but they were counted as being trustworthy and reliable. Let us always remember the words of our Lord in John 20:17:

> "...Go to *My brethren* and say to them, 'I am ascending to My Father and your Father, and to My God and your God.'"

Furthermore, in Hebrews 2:11 we read:

> "For both He who sanctifies and those who are

being sanctified are all of one, for which reason he is not ashamed to call them *brethren*".

Paul then greets them with a desire that "grace" should be given to them from God the Father. God our Father is the spring and source of every blessing. Paul reminds them that the all-powerful, all-knowing, unchanging, ever-present God is now active for them as Father. As the Father then, He must (because of who He is) do what is best for His own. So grace, that is, 'divine favour', flows from Him to these Christians at Colossae.

Yet Paul would couple this grace with "peace" because one complements the other. The word "peace" speaks of harmonious relationships between us and God and, also, us and one another. Our God is the *source* of peace (Romans 15:33). We also know that we have peace *with* God because Christ has borne the judgment against our sins (Romans 5:1). Furthermore, we know the peace *of* God (Philippians 4:7; Colossians 3:15). That is to say, we have such confidence in the God of peace that we can be at rest in the varied circumstances of life. The act of worrying is a sin. It shows a lack of dependence upon God. Knowing God as our Father, we can cast all our care upon Him as simply as throwing a garment over the back of a donkey (compare 1 Peter 5:7 and Luke 19:35).

COLOSSIANS 1:3-6 — PAUL'S GRATITUDE FOR THEIR FAITH, LOVE, HOPE AND FRUITFULNESS

The Apostle, along with others, is found thanking God for the Colossians as well as constantly praying for them. Prayer makes request, while thanksgiving is the return of praise for requests answered. Those who praise or thank God are offering up spiritual sacrifices and giving the honour or glory to Him. The words "the God and Father of our Lord Jesus Christ" tell us that the same Father loves us even to the degree that He loves His own beloved Son. It is in Him that all the Father's counsels and purposes will be fulfilled. The expression is used six times in the New Testament showing the Father to be the Subject of glory and praise (Romans 15:6); the Searcher of hearts (2 Corinthians 11:31); the Selector of those in Christ (Ephesians 1:3-4); the Comforter (2 Corinthians 1:3); and the merciful One who has secured our future (1 Peter 1:3).

Like Paul, we may find fresh causes for which we can thank God for our fellow believers. The *faith* of the Colossian Christians, their *love* towards all other believers, and the *hope* they possessed are the three reasons given for Paul's thanksgiving. Interestingly, Paul had heard these things witnessed about the Colossians. They could not be classed as secret or passive disciples. They made, as we all should, the confession of their faith known. Is the testimony of our local church as commendable? Furthermore, do we, like Paul, give thanks for those whom we know fully trust in the exalted Saviour and act accordingly? Do we give thanks for those whose love for *all* their fellow believers reflects the universal love of God? Do we give thanks that Christians are encouraged by that sure hope, namely, an inheritance secured for them in heaven? Peter describes it as —

> "an inheritance incorruptible and undefiled and that does not fade away, reserved in heaven for you" (1 Peter 1:4).

It is therefore an inheritance which is both indestructible and pure, and one which retains its value eternally.

This triad of virtues (faith, love and hope) marks the life of the Christian. Faith rests in Christ and all that He has done and is doing. Love works in and through our hearts today. Hope looks to certainty in the future.

Paul reminds the Colossians that they had heard of this hope previously, perhaps when Epaphras (verse 7) preached the Gospel to them. Paul describes this as "the word of the truth of the gospel" (verse 5) which emphasizes the *truth* of the good news that they had received as opposed to the *false* teachings that were, at that time, infiltrating their company.

In verse 6, the Apostle states that the word of the truth of the Gospel "has come to you, as it has also in all the world". The Greek word for "has come" [literally, "is come"] is *pareimi* which is usually reserved for the coming of a person. It emphasizes the fact that the glad tidings concern the Person of Christ. The fact that Paul refers to all the world, shows that the range of the Gospel was universal. What had been experienced at Colossae was happening everywhere the Gospel was preached. The Revised Version reads:

"Which is come unto you; even as it is also in all the world, bearing fruit and increasing".

This translation highlights the supernatural power of the Gospel because a plant does not naturally bear fruit and increase at the same time. Usually, it has to be pruned to be fruitful or else it grows wild with all of its life being drained in the growth of branches and leaves. The Gospel was bearing fruit in the salvation of souls *and* increasing in the growth of these new Christians spiritually.

The expression "the grace of God in truth" reminds the Colossians that it is the undeserved favour of God that the Gospel exhibits. It is God's sovereign display of love which saves and sanctifies those who believe. This is in contrast

13

to the false teaching that a person's own, so-called good works or keeping of rules and ordinances are able to save them.

COLOSSIANS 1:7-8 — PAUL'S APPRECIATION OF EPAPHRAS

Firstly, Epaphras was a teacher. We can see this in the words "as you also learned..." He had brought the Gospel message to the Colossians and had nurtured it so that it affected their lives substantially. The Apostle describes him as a "dear fellow-servant". This, and what follows, sets the seal of approval upon what Epaphras was teaching. As a fellow-servant or bondslave then, his position in Christ was the same as that of Paul and Timothy. They were bondslaves to the same Master. Therefore, his teaching and life was geared to the word of the Lord. Note too, that Epaphras was *dear* to them. He was both highly esteemed and loved. Furthermore, he is described as a "faithful minister on your [or, "our", RV] behalf". As a representative of Paul to the Colossians, Epaphras was commended for his reliability and trustworthiness. It was also Epaphras who carried the report of their love in the Spirit to the Apostle. This love is not merely human affection, but a genuine love which always seeks the best for the Lord and His people. It was a love promoted by the indwelling Spirit of God.

COLOSSIANS 1:9-11 — PAUL'S INTERCESSION FOR THEIR SPIRITUAL GROWTH

In this section, Paul's prayers for the Christians at Colossae express an abundance which can be seen in his use of the words 'all' and 'every'.

KNOW GOD'S WILL

Firstly, he wanted them to be "filled with the knowledge of [God's] will in all wisdom and spiritual understanding". The Holy Spirit will give the spiritual insight whereby we can understand the will of God for our lives through God's word. Wisdom is the application of that understanding to our lives. Romans 12:2 shows us that obedience to His word will prove His will to be good, acceptable and perfect.

WALK WORTHILY

Secondly, he wanted their walk, that is, the course and conduct of their lives, to give pleasure to God just as the life of the Lord Jesus could draw forth the Father's expression of delight – "This is My beloved Son, in whom I am well pleased" (Matthew 3:17; 17:5).

WORK FRUITFULLY

Thirdly, they were to do good works. A good work is one which is done to benefit others while giving the credit to God alone. His glory is the motive for good works. Only those who are new creatures in Christ are capable of doing good works (Ephesians 2:10 and Titus 3:8).

GROW IN THE KNOWLEDGE OF GOD

Fourthly, Paul wanted them to increase in the knowledge of God. The only way to do this is through communion with Him in prayer, studying His revealed word and living in His will (Hosea 6:3).

BE EMPOWERED TO PATIENCE

Fifthly, he wanted them to be "strengthened with all might, according to His glorious power, for all patience and longsuffering with joy". This power is tapped by prayer. The purpose for it is *not* to create marvellous preachers or the working of miracles, but rather to produce joyfulness in our lives when we are under great trial. "Patience" is a word which speaks of endurance under pressure and "long-suffering" expresses a quiet suffering of the failings of others or their abuse. Thomas Bentley writes that " 'Patience' means 'no giving-up', 'longsuffering' infers 'no giving-back', while 'with joyfulness' suggests 'no giving-in' " (*What the Bible Teaches: Colossians*).

EXPRESS A THANKFUL SPIRIT

Finally, Paul wants them to have thankful hearts in the light of what the Father has done for them. Oh that our Christian lives might register these qualities also!

COLOSSIANS 1:12-13 — THE FATHER'S WORK

Verse 12 introduces us to the Father's work. Like the Colossians, we can give thanks to the Father for making us suitable to be sharers in the inheritance of the saints in light. It is the blood of Christ in completely atoning for our sins which has made us fit for the presence of God — He who dwells in unapproachable light. Paul also shows us we are saints, as discussed previously. Light speaks of the presence and the glory of God. The light of the knowledge of His glory is seen in the face of Jesus Christ. When we are with Christ, then we shall know the brightness of that glory. Therefore, I suggest that the inheritance referred to here is nothing less than the Lord Jesus Christ Himself just as the LORD was the inheritance of Levi (Deuteronomy 10:9). It is an inheritance common to all real Christians and, to some degree, may be enjoyed now.

Moreover, verse 13 tells us that the Father has rescued us from the domain of Satan and "translated us into the kingdom of the Son of His love" (RV). The word "translated" signifies conquerors capturing whole nations and taking them to distant lands. It reminds us of the Lord Jesus Christ who —

"through death He might destroy him who had the power of death, that is, the devil, and release those who through fear of death were all their lifetime subject to bondage" (Hebrews 2:14-15).

So from the realm of darkness, danger and death we have been brought into a kingdom of light, love and life. Our rulers are no longer Satan and Sin, but the Son of the Father's love and Righteousness. The Son of the Father's love is the Lord Jesus Christ who is both the *object* of the Father's love and the *revealer* of it. Matthew 3:17 and 17:5 inform us that the love of the Father for the Son is unoriginated and uninterrupted.

COLOSSIANS 1:14-18 — THE GLORIES OF CHRIST IN RELATION TO GOD, CREATION, THE CHURCH AND ALL THINGS

In verse 14 the glories of Christ begin to emerge.

Firstly, He is, as we have seen already in verse 13, the Son of the Father's love. The Divine relationship between the Father and the Son prior to His entry into the world, during His manhood here on earth, and now in glory is indicated by the verses that follow.

Secondly, He is the Son "in whom we have redemption, the forgiveness of sins." This means that we are in union with the Son of the Father who has released us from bondage to sin and death by the payment of a ransom. He was made sin on our account. He suffered that terrible punishment of death. We hear it in His cry from the cross, "My God, my God, why have You forsaken Me?" (Matthew 27:46). In Matthew 20:28 we read:

"just as the Son of Man did not come to be served, but to serve, and to give His life a ransom for many."

17

Christians are ransomed in this way as soon as they trust in Christ. We are assured that we will never come under God's sword of judgement against sin.

Aphesin is the Greek word meaning "forgiveness" here. It may also mean "to send away". In our union with the Son our sins are dismissed so that they may never again be called against us. Therefore, we cannot be enslaved by Satan, the "accuser of our brethren" (Revelation 12:10), ever again. It is God who justifies us through the work of His Son.

Thirdly, the expression "He is the image of the invisible God" shows us that the Son of the Father's love is not just a divine copy or even a visible representation; but a real, essential embodiment of God. This is a proof of the Deity of Christ because only God could perfectly reveal God. The words "who is" suggest a continuance as such. The Son is the visible representation and manifestation of God to created beings. In John 1:18 we find,

> "No one has seen God at any time. The only begotten Son, who is in the bosom of the Father, He has declared Him."

Here He declares God, while in John 14:9, He reveals God as Father:

> "He who has seen Me has seen the Father".

Fourthly, the Son is presented to us as the "Firstborn over all creation". The word "firstborn" in this verse denotes honour, rank or dignity. It tells us that the Son is pre-eminent over all creation. It shows priority of *position* rather than that of *time*. So, even when the Son became a man, creation, as it were, lay at His feet. In verse 16, we immediately read that all things were created by Him. This is better translated as "in Him were all things created" (RV). This means that He is the Source and Architect of creation. The power to create was in His Being. Every sphere of creation is then mentioned whether the heavens and the earth, things visible and invisible, along with all forms of power and rule. The end of the verse tells us that "all things were created through [or, "by", N.Tr.] Him and for Him." This pinpoints two facts. Firstly, that the Son was the Person of the Godhead who performed the creative act and, secondly, that the Son is the One on whose account all things were created. They were created for His possession, pleasure and glory. The whole verse emphasizes the fact that Christ is Superior to all other beings and things because they are the created and He the Eternal, the Creator.

Verse 17 stresses this in the words "And He *is* before all things". The present tense is used to show the timelessness of Deity. The Son *is* God! An example of this is found in John 8:58 where Christ says, "Before Abraham was, I AM." Compare this with Exodus 3:14 where God declares His name to be "I AM WHO I AM" and instructs Moses to tell the people that "I AM" had sent him to them. The Lord Jesus Christ claimed to be the Jehovah of the Old Testament. He claimed to be God.

Not only was He before all, but "by Him all things consist" (verse 17, RV). The whole universe is sustained by the Son of the Father's love. As Hebrews 1:3 indicates, He is "upholding all things by the word of His power".

It is a power which He demonstrated on earth when He calmed the storm with the words, "Peace, be still." Paul wanted to focus the attention of the Colossian Christians upon the Son of the Father's love. May this be our daily focus, in order that God may fill our hearts with His peace in the face of all opposition.

Colossians 1:19–2:3
Christ in you the hope of glory

BY DOUGLAS PETTMAN

My wife recently asked me to buy a particular type of cleaning fluid. As I scanned the supermarket shelves I found the brand name and duly bought a bottle. Yes, it was the correct brand; my wife claimed it was an excellent cleansing agent, but it was just not suitable for the job in hand. Another product from the same manufacturer was required. Happily, in speaking of spiritual matters, we find that the Lord Jesus is not only the most excellent Person to meet our need but He provides for every condition and circumstance. Our further consideration of this lovely letter to the Colossians will show this to be so.

Before we look at this passage, let us remind ourselves of the purpose of the letter. The Apostle Paul wrote it at a time when erroneous teaching was spreading in the church of God as a whole and the church at Colossae was similarly under attack. Further, a system of teaching, known as Gnosticism, was beginning to be introduced, and this church would also have been troubled by it. The word 'Gnosticism' means 'knowledge'; these people said, 'I know', but their teaching was far from the truth.

Amongst other things, they denied the Deity of the Lord Jesus Christ and His work of redemption. Thus, the matter was so serious that the Apostle deals with these things in his letter. It is most interesting to note that Paul does not try to deal with specific allegations which are raised but, rather, he takes the positive approach to these matters with clear positive statements. This leads to the great point: Christ is all we need, all our future is bound up with Him.

We learned in the first part of the chapter of the twofold Headship of Christ: the Headship of Creation and the Headship of the Church. We will see, as we go on, two more pairs also linked with creation and the Church. These are:

• The twofold *reconciliation* (verses 20-22): the reconciliation of all things (in creation) and our reconciliation (the Church), and,

• Paul's twofold *ministry* (verses 23-29): the ministry of the Gospel (preached in all creation), and ministry to the Church (to present every man perfect in Christ).

COLOSSIANS 1:19 — THE INCOMPARABLE HEAD

Who is it who has these Headships? Who is it that is able to bring reconciliation? Paul has to bring in here the full nature of the Person, the Lord Jesus Christ, of whom he is speaking. "For in Him all the fullness was pleased to dwell" (N.Tr.). The New King James Version (following the King James Version) says, "it pleased the Father". This addition was supplied to try to assist the understanding but, if it is used, it should really refer to 'the Godhead', not just 'the Father'.

To help us understand this statement we can refer to 2:9:

"For in Him dwells all the fullness of the Godhead bodily".

So here is a direct statement of His Deity. "All the fullness of the Godhead" includes the Father, the Son and the Holy Spirit. In John 14:9-10, the Lord Jesus says,

"He who has seen Me has seen the Father; ... I am in the Father, and the Father in Me".

We also read His words in John 3:34,

"For He whom God has sent speaks the words of God, for God does not give the Spirit by measure."

There was not just 'a measure' of the Holy Spirit with the Lord Jesus but the Spirit was in Him in all fullness. All the fullness was pleased to dwell in Him.

The term 'fullness' also is interesting. The Gnostics gave it a true meaning of absolute perfection of deity. Their trouble was that they would not allow this to be applied to Christ. However, Paul, in his glorious way, reminds the Colossians that in the Lord Jesus Christ was absolute perfection of Deity, in whom Father, Son and Holy Spirit, were pleased to dwell. The One who has the headship in creation, the headship of the Church, the only One who displayed the Father in all His perfection in this world, is none other than the Lord Jesus Christ. Thus, in our day, we can rejoice both in the Deity and completeness of the One who has so cared for us, and in no one else.

COLOSSIANS 1:20-22 — THE TWO RECONCILIATIONS

So, having established the Person, the Apostle is able to go on to His work. In these verses we now learn of the two reconciliations. The term 'reconciliation' includes the bringing together of two opposed parties to the point of understanding and agreement. How is it possible for this to be done? The very One who displayed all the fullness of the Godhead, who ever blessed and met every need, was the One whom man rejected and hated without a cause. In spite of all that man was and is, God had determined to reconcile man with Himself. At the very time when man would finally demonstrate all his hatred against the Lord Jesus by crucifying Him on the Cross, God would display, through the Lord Jesus, the wonder of His everlasting love and great grace. It was at the cross, through the blood of His cross, that He made peace. Here was the place of reconciliation, the place where peace was made.

IN ALL CREATION

In verse 20 we can first note that, through the cross, there is a reconciliation of all things to Himself, in earth or in heaven. This is the first reconciliation. It includes all creation and the whole universe. When Adam sinned, the whole world was plunged into disarray.

We live now in a groaning world, Romans 8:21-22 tells us. All is in disorder. Satan and his wicked spirits are in the heavens and there is defilement there. But all the power of evil will be defeated. Through "the blood of His cross" all will be restored when the Lord comes again and all things are put "in subjection under His feet" (Hebrews 2:8; 1 Corinthians 15:25).

We have a reference to this in Acts 3:19-21, where Peter speaks of —

> "times of refreshing may come from the presence of the Lord, and that He may send Jesus Christ, who was preached to you before, whom Heaven must receive until the times of restoration of all things,

which God has spoken by the mouth of all His holy prophets since the world began."

So the Old Testament prophets also spoke of this. For instance, look at Isaiah 11:6-9, where harmony is restored.

"The wolf also shall dwell with the lamb, ... The cow and the bear shall graze; ... The earth shall be full of the knowledge of the LORD as the waters cover the sea."

What a wonderful time is coming for the whole earth in that day of the reign of the Lord Jesus over this world!

It may well be asked if the unsaved are included in this reconciliation. These are they who have previously rejected "the blood of His cross" and remain in their sins. There is no suggestion in the Scriptures of the possibility of reconciliation then, only a pleading to men *now* to be reconciled with God (2 Corinthians 5:20). The blessing of God in reconciliation through Christ is the point of our chapter and verse 20 refers to "things on earth or things in heaven".

When there is a question of obedience to His authority, this is a different matter. Then we read in Philippians 2:10 that —

"every knee should bow, of those in heaven, and of those on earth, and of those under the earth".

Here those "under the earth" are included and must give honour, although they remain in their sins. Their destination is everlasting punishment and no future reconciliation is found in the Word of God.

RECONCILIATION FOR BELIEVERS (THE CHURCH).

While the earth is awaiting the reconciliation of all things, there is a second reconciliation referred to in verses 21-22.

> "And you, who once were alienated and enemies in your mind by wicked works, yet now He has reconciled in the body of His flesh through death, to present you holy, and blameless, and above reproach in His sight".

How vastly different this is for those who have already believed on the Lord Jesus Christ, including believers today. What assurance it brings! Reconciliation has already been made. We were enemies once, but no longer. Once, because of our sins, we could look forward only to eternal punishment, but now we are reconciled. We are seen as "blameless and above reproach". God Himself only sees the work of Christ, "the blood of His cross", and everyone who has trusted the Lord Jesus as Saviour is reconciled for ever.

In reconciliation, God has come to a *judicial* peace with us; we have come to a *submissive* peace with God. Are we thankful today for all that our Saviour has done for us? This tremendous achievement has been brought about by the One whom Paul has shown to have full Deity, God Himself, and this brings with it the full satisfaction which only God can offer.

There are words of caution in verse 23. The verse reads,

> "If indeed you continue in the faith, grounded and steadfast, and are not moved away from the hope of the gospel which you heard..."

Every believer who has been reconciled will continue in the faith and will not be moved away. However, there are many who hear the Gospel and know that it is true but reject and turn away from its truth. By this they show that they were never truly reconciled in the first place.

We now come on to:

COLOSSIANS 1:23-29 — THE TWO MINISTRIES

THE GOSPEL – IN ALL CREATION (VERSE 23)

One of the responsibilities the Apostle had been given by God Himself was to preach the Gospel. To do so, he had travelled far through the civilised world of his day. To him the Gospel included not only the good news of salvation but covered the good news of the full eternal blessing of all believers everywhere leading into the blessings in glory. Yet how vital to the Apostle that people everywhere come to a knowledge of the Lord Jesus Christ as Saviour. All other Bible teaching is of no value unless it leads to a settlement of the matter of sin. Only the 'good news' of the Gospel will make the difference. Therefore he was concerned that it be "preached to every creature under heaven". He was made a minister of this Gospel. Is this a ministry you are exercising too?

THE MINISTRY CONCERNING THE CHURCH (VERSES 24-29)

The Apostle also tells us in verse 25 that he "became a minister" "to fulfill the word of God." He tells us what this involved. Preaching the Gospel and teaching the truth of "the mystery", as he calls it in verse 26, cost him dearly in troubles and afflictions. He lists some of these in 2 Corinthians 11:23-30. He believes suffering to be necessary to make the sorrows of Christ complete. This does not mean that the work of Christ on the Cross was in any way incomplete, but the servant of Christ has his part in knowing something of suffering when active on the work of his Lord.

More important than his own suffering, Paul also tells us what the teaching involved. It concerned "the mystery", he says,

> "which has been hidden from ages and from generations, but now has been revealed to His saints" (verse 26).

We need to understand this mystery.

THE MYSTERY

First, a mystery, in the biblical usage of the word, is something that was unknown but is now made known. This mystery was unknown throughout the Old Testament period but has now been made known to New Testament 'saints', that is, all who have believed in the work of the Lord Jesus at Calvary and have been separated to Christ. It is not restricted to the Jewish nation; it has been made known to Gentiles also. Then we learn that it concerns the Lord Jesus Christ. What is this mystery?

We learn, in the Old Testament, of prophecies concerning the coming of the Lord Jesus, His birth, His life, His death, His resurrection, His coming to reign. So the mystery is none of these. The Apostle says,

> "God willed to make known what are the riches of the glory of this mystery among the Gentiles: which is Christ in you, the hope of glory" (verse 27).

Paul describes this as "the riches of the glory of this mystery". It is so wonderful; it abounds with the blessing of God. So what has been provided? God has seen fit now to make known, since the death and resurrection of the Lord Jesus, the truth concerning the Church of God. The Lord Jesus, as Head, in heaven, gathers in one body on earth, all believers whether Jew or Gentile. All are one in

Him as the Church on earth, as Paul writes, "Christ in you, the hope of glory."

Everything looks forward to the final consummation – in glory – where the 'body' will be with the 'Head'. The whole purpose of the Apostle is to *warn* every one of the consequences of missing out on the blessings, and *teach* every one of the great blessings provided by God that we may be wise and perfect. This word 'perfect' brings the thought of being 'mature' or 'full grown'. When we really get a grasp of what the Lord has done we take on a fuller character of a true Christian in this world. This was so important to the Apostle that he actively laboured to this end.

COLOSSIANS 2:1-3 — REASONS FOR HIS WORK

In the beginning of chapter 2, Paul speaks of some reasons for writing. It seems that those in Laodicea and Colossae had never seen the Apostle. But he happily includes you and me here too when he writes, "as many as have not seen my face in the flesh". The understanding of this 'mystery' is of such vital and valuable importance that its truth must be constantly asserted. It must never be overlooked. False teaching was bound to come but should never be allowed to replace that which is right. So Paul refers to the possibility —

"lest anyone should deceive you with persuasive words" (verse 4).

May we never lose the joy of knowing all that God has purposed for the future.

But there is another reason for his writing. There was "a great conflict", an anxiety within him that, without the understanding of this wonderful truth, there would be much missing. But in the learning of it the believers would be so "encouraged". Their hearts "being knit together in love", that is, having put these things together in their minds, their love would abound. This is what a full understanding would bring.

God has done so much for each one of us. May we seize these truths again today and be refreshed in the knowledge that we have been reconciled to Him. May the provision He has made of placing each one of us, as believers, within the One Body of the Church, linked with our Lord in Heaven, thrill us again. May we look forward with longing to the moment when all will be complete. We shall be together with Him in the soon-coming day. What a day that will be!

Colossians 2:4-23
You are complete in Him

BY ERNIE BROWN

The Apostle Paul was a good teacher. First, he commends what is commendable. He starts from a point on which there is common agreement. He then uses that as a springboard for further progress. This comes through clearly in this portion of the letter.

THE FOUR PREPOSITIONS

Many years ago, I attended a Bible discussion group on this scripture. The opening statement was this. "The teaching of Colossians 2 hangs upon four prepositions." Quick as a flash, a very earnest Christian gentleman, much used of God in the preaching of the Gospel, jumped in. He was always very direct. His eyes twinkled as he said, "Can I learn the teaching of this chapter if I don't know what a preposition is?" I cannot remember the actual answer given. I do remember that he was assured that every Christian is able to learn all that he needs to know, even if he isn't familiar with some of the more technical terms some people use. However, for those who are interested, and are not put off by the words, it is certainly true to say that the teaching of this chapter is crystallized in the use made of four prepositions included in the text.

To get our bearings, chapter 1 teaches us that primarily, the basis and focal point of Christianity is the person of our Lord Jesus Christ, and the value to God of the work of the Lord Jesus upon the cross of Calvary.

Basically, chapter 2 tells us about what is true *of* the Christian and *for* the Christian because of their *relationship to*, and *association with*, the Lord Jesus Christ. This teaching can be summarised under four headings taken from the text itself:

1. In verse 11, we are told, "*In* Him you were also circumcised".
2. In verse 12, we are "buried *with* Him in baptism".
3. In verse 17, "the substance is *of* Christ."
4. In verse 19, "the Head, *from* whom all the body, nourished and knit together by joints and ligaments, grows with the increase that is from God."

Putting it even more succinctly, the teaching is concentrated into what we are —

1. in Him,

2. with Him,

3. of Him,

and what we receive —

4. from Him.

Hence the reference to the four prepositions.

JEWISH ORDINANCES AND GRECIAN PHILOSOPHY

Why is the teaching concentrated in this way? The Colossian Christians were exposed to a two-pronged attack. Verse 8 says,

"Beware lest anyone cheat you through philosophy and empty deceit, according to the tradition of men, according to the basic principles of the world, and not according to Christ."

First of all, in verses 16-17, Paul says,

"So let no one judge you in food or in drink, or regarding a festival or a new moon or sabbaths, which are a shadow of things to come".

That is, there were those who tried to tell them that Christianity involved keeping to a set of rules, in particular, Jewish ordinances.

Secondly, we read in verse 18,

"Let no one cheat you of your reward, taking delight in false humility and worship of angels, intruding into those things which he has not seen, vainly puffed up by his fleshly mind".

That is, don't be deceived by Grecian philosophy. What these philosophers said sounded quite reasonable to those brought up under a Greek culture. This seemed to be their line of reasoning:

God is so great, so majestic, so powerful, so infinite in His person, that mere man, well down the scale of created beings, could not possibly know God in person. In between God and man, they said, there are various steps and stairs of intermediate beings, greater than man, but less than God. They claimed to be in touch with these intermediate beings, principalities and powers, as the Bible terms them. The most dangerous part of their philosophy was that concerning the Lord Jesus Christ Himself. They recognized that He was much more than an ordinary man. They agreed that He was the greatest Person in the universe apart from God.

But that was their great error. It is not sufficient to say that He is almost but not quite God. He *is* God, in Person, and there is none greater. The marvel is that He who is really God became a real man. He voluntarily entered into a condition in which it was possible for Him to die. (Read Hebrews 2:9.)

To put the Letter to the Colossians into perspective, there are two vital statements in the text.

- 1:19 – "in Him all the fullness was pleased to dwell" (N.Tr.). That is, the Lord Jesus is no less glorious in Person having become a man than He was before He became a man, in what we may call abstract Deity.

- 2:9 – "in Him dwells all the fullness of the Godhead bodily". That is, now He has gone back to heaven as a man, He is no less a person than He ever was: whether in Deity before He came into the world, or when He lived in the world as a real man. These are tremendous concepts we do well to think about and pray over.

COLOSSIANS 2:4-10 — DEEPER MYSTERIES?

Another major error pressed upon the Colossian Christians was along these lines:

Jesus is a great and wonderful person. Not quite God, but a great person nevertheless. In coming to Him, the Colossians had done well, really well. However, they, the Grecian philosophers, could teach the Christians much more wonderful things and explain to them even more wonderful mysteries, if only the Colossians would accept that there was much more they needed to learn which only these philosophers could teach them.

This is where the Apostle Paul had to step in and put his foot down. "Just a minute," he said. "Hold on. That can't be right." He went right back to the beginning. "You are Christians. You have received Christ, by faith. You certainly have much to learn. But you will only make progress by continuing in the same way you began." Verse 6 says,

> "As you have therefore received the Lord Jesus, so walk in Him."

How had they received Him? As the only One who could meet their need! At that time, their greatest need was to have their sins forgiven. As the One who had died for their sins, He was the only One who could do that. And He had, for everyone who trusted Him as Saviour and confessed Him as Lord. That was the greatest need they would ever have, the need of salvation. And He had fully met that need.

Now Paul says, "The One who met your greatest need is well equipped to meet every other need you will ever have. There is nothing you really need that He cannot supply, if you live in full dependence upon Him. There He is, in heaven, the mighty God, and a real man. He is all-glorious. There is nothing He cannot do. Everything you could ever need is found in Him." "You are complete in Him", as verse 10 tells us.

The philosophers said, "We are in touch with great beings, principalities and powers. Come to us. We will teach you." Paul says, "Jesus is the head of all principality and power. He controls them all. Why be over-concerned with lesser beings when you are in touch with the Greatest of all beings?" At best, the principalities and powers are created beings. The Lord Jesus is the Creator and Sustainer of all creation, and every creature in it.

COLOSSIANS 2:11-19 — COMPLETE IN HIM

Having put that into proper perspective, Paul then expounds in more detail what he meant in verse 10 when he said, "You are complete in Him." Before we look at the detail, there is a very important factor we must consider. It is one thing to say, "You are complete in Him." That, in itself, implies, "You cannot be complete without Him." In other words, if you leave Him out of your life, you can never live a full life. There will always be something lacking. Christ personally is absolutely vital to the life of the committed Christian. This is where the four prepositions of chapter 2 come in, highlighting what we have as Christian believers in virtue of our links, our association with our Lord Jesus Christ.

CUT OFF

First of all, then, let us look at verse 11 of our chapter.

> "*In* Him you were also circumcised with the circumcision made without hands, by putting off the body of the sins of the flesh, by the circumcision of Christ."

Circumcision is a clean cut, a complete cutting off. It was a sign given to the people of Israel to confirm to them that God had cut them off completely from Egypt. Pharaoh no longer had any claim upon them. God had delivered them once and for all from the power of Egypt and Pharaoh. (See Joshua 5:2-9 and also Genesis 17:9-14.) The application is clear. Sin and Satan no longer have any real claim on the Christian. Why? Because, in the sight of God, the Christian has been cut off completely from their sins, and the penalty due because of them, but not in virtue of anything the Christian is in themself or anything they have done for themselves.

The cutting off is in virtue of the cutting off of Christ, in death, upon the cross of Calvary. Does scripture say so? Yes, indeed! Remember Psalm 102:24,

> "Do not take me away [*do not cut me off*] in the midst of my days".

This was the cry prophetically attributed to the Lord as He anticipated the cross. In the garden of Gethsemane, He prayed,

> "Father, save Me from this hour? But for this purpose I came to this hour. Father, glorify Your Name" (John 12:27-28).

But scripture had already said in Isaiah 53:8,

> "He was cut off from the land of the living".

Then, in Daniel 9:26, we read,

> "Messiah shall be cut off".

So, in God's judgement, all who trust Christ as Saviour have been cut off, severed completely, by God, from all fear of penalty for their sins. Colossians 2:11 could well be paraphrased, "You are cut off from the judgement of God because Christ was cut off in death on your behalf at Calvary." Christ has borne the burden, paid the price, discharged the debt, accepted the punishment on their behalf. Now there is no fear of judgement for those who trust in Christ.

BAPTISM

Secondly, verse 12 reads,

> "buried *with* Him in baptism, in which you also were raised *with* Him through faith in the working of God, who raised Him from the dead."

If circumcision is a complete cutting off, baptism is a going out of sight, as when a body is buried. Baptism identifies us with Christ in His death. It symbolises the fact that, in God's sight, the old life, the life of sin, has been brought to a complete end in the death of Christ. Further, in so far as we are linked with Christ who is risen from among the dead, we now have a new life to live which glorifies God, and a new power, the power of the Holy Spirit, in which and by which to live it. How graphic the picture is!

SHADOW AND SUBSTANCE

Thirdly, verses 14 to 17 tell us that Jewish ordinances are but

> "a shadow of things to come, but the substance is *of* Christ."

There is as much difference between Judaism and Christianity as between shadow and substance. There is a well-known and well-founded expression, "Coming events cast their shadow before them." God allows things to happen which give us an idea of things which, in their fullness, God will bring in, or allow to happen, later. Paul says here, "Don't be put off by the shadowy outline which is Judaism. Enjoy the reality and fullness found in Christ." There again, this feature of the Colossian letter comes through. Christ is the fullness of God, in the glory of His own person. All fullness resides in Him.

HOLD FAST TO THE HEAD

Fourthly, in verse 19, Paul exhorts the Colossians to

"holding fast to the Head, *from* whom all the body, nourished and knit together by joints and ligaments, grows with the increase that is from God."

This is one of the most important statements in the letter. Paul puts it in a negative way, pointing out the folly of "not holding fast to the Head", in reality exhorting them to "hold fast to the Head". What does that involve? Something like this. Christ is our Head. We have put ourselves under His control. He has every resource at His command. He makes them all available to us if we will come to Him and receive them from Him. As a plant needs regular, sustained nourishment to grow and develop, so the Christian can and must grow and develop spiritually. To do so, spiritual nourishment must be drawn from Christ Himself, no doubt in the power of the Holy Spirit, through the agency of the Word of God. As we encourage the children to sing:

> *"Read your Bible,*
> *Pray every day,*
> *And you'll grow."*

COLOSSIANS 2:20-23 — CHRIST IS EVERYTHING

Finally, the chapter ends with Paul reminding the Colossians, and us, not to waste time on lesser things, or lesser beings. Christ is *everything* to the Christian. He is the Source and Provider of everything we could ever rightly desire. Let us not be satisfied with less than the best. As the poet (Mrs Mary Jane Walker [née Deck]) said, *"I have Christ, what want I more?"*

Spiritual growth in a Christian is like physical growth in a baby or a child. Take a balanced diet of good wholesome food, take a reasonable amount of suitable exercise, and growth and development will take place. We may not understand all the processes involved. Most of us do not know or understand the long technical terms used by the experts. But putting into practice a system which has been proved to work, it will happen. Again, I say,

> *"Read your Bible,*
> *Pray every day,*
> *And you'll grow."*

SUMMARY

Pulling together, then, the teaching of Colossians 2:4-23, we have this:

- Christ is God. Christ is man. Christ is alive in heaven.

- Christ is absolutely essential to every Christian. We cannot manage without Him. Indeed, without Him we *have* nothing and we *are* nothing.

- Because we have trusted Christ as Saviour, and confessed Him as Lord, God has accepted the death of Christ as being on our behalf. We need have no fear in respect of the day of judgement. Every one of our sins has been blotted out.

- In God's sight, our old life of sin has been brought to an end in the death of Christ. Because Christ is alive from among the dead, a new way of life has been opened up for us and to us.

- We don't need any of the religious or philosophical paraphernalia of this world to bolster our spiritual lives. Christ is everything. If we have Him, potentially we have everything. All we need finds its source and origin in Him.

- He is the willing provider of all that we might ever need. We draw from Him all that we need to promote our spiritual health, prosperity, growth and development.

God grant that we draw freely, from Christ, all we shall ever need, and give God the praise and worship from grateful hearts.

Colossians 3:1-17
Christ our life

BY GEORGE BELL

Some time ago a question was raised on a radio programme, "What is your life?" There are many absorbing subjects which almost take over the lives of men and women in our day. Just think of the hold sport has over the minds of men, old and young alike. Just listen to conversations when travelling on the bus, or listening to people in the street, the topic is football! What a grip it has on the mind. It is their life! With others it may be politics; with another it may be the business world; and so we could go on. It would be worthwhile quietly to sift through and analyse our lives and ask ourselves, "What is my life?"

This question needs to be faced by all believers in the Lord Jesus Christ. There are legitimate things we must give our minds to; many of us have our homes and our families to occupy much of our time. All areas must, however, pale into nothing as we think of our subject: "Christ our life".

41

COLOSSIANS 3:1-4 — "A GOLDEN PARAGRAPH"

We will first of all consider verses 1-4. Just recently I read an exposition of the Letter to the Colossians in which the writer referred to these 4 verses as "a golden paragraph" (H. C. G.Moule, *Lessons in Faith and Holiness from St Paul's Epistles to the Colossians and Philemon*).

RAISED WITH CHRIST

It is obvious that the writer bases these four verses on the teaching of chapter 2 in which all believers are regarded as "raised with [Christ]" (2:12) and also "dead with Christ" (2:20). Believers have not attained to this through any effort of their own. It is by virtue of their union with Christ. So chapter 3 begins, "If then you were raised with Christ..." The 'if' does not convey any element of doubt. It may be clearer to read the words, "Since then you were raised with Christ". Paul follows on with a call,

"seek those things which are above, where Christ is, sitting at the right hand of God."

The 'things above' are the spiritual riches and blessings belonging to every believer through Christ and because of His death.

The letter to the Colossians was written to counter wrong teaching which tended to give Christ an inferior place. This will never do! Further down the chapter, in verse 11, the Apostle writes, "Christ is everything" (N.Tr.). Do you really believe that? Does He have this place in your heart and life? We all have to confess sadly that other things crowd Him out. What a challenge! No other person or even an angelic being is ever said to be "sitting at the right hand of God". It belongs to Christ because of who He is. Though He be so great, yet He has won our hearts. What an object to attract the Christian away from the things on earth!

Verse 2 carries on the theme:

"Set your *mind* on things above, not on things on the earth."

Much is said in the New Testament letters about the mind. Romans 12:2 and Ephesians 4:23 speak of renewed minds. There is a discipline needed here to set our minds in the right direction, as they are prone to wander. Whatever occupies the mind affects the heart and will alter our behaviour. Let's not focus our attention on things that do not profit, but on things that pay spiritual dividends.

HIDDEN WITH CHRIST

Moving further down this "golden paragraph" we consider verse 3.

"For you died, and your life is hidden with Christ in God."

Our life is hidden and as yet there is no public display of the glory of Christ. It will not always be so. The chorus of a well known hymn says, *"Oh, the crowning day is coming, is coming by and by"*. We are sure of this. In the meantime our faith and our patience are put to the test. There is a telling illustration of this in the Old Testament. It is found in 2 Kings 11.

They were turbulent days in the kingdom of Judah. On the death of king Ahaziah his mother, Athaliah, usurped the throne. She was a wicked woman and in order to feed her ambition she killed all the royal children. These were really her grandchildren. It looked bad for the royal line of David. However, one of the children was preserved from her destroying hand, only a baby it would seem. The wife of Jehoiada the priest took the boy and hid him in the temple of the LORD. He was hidden for six years; very few knew about it. After the six years, the king was shown to the army chiefs. They were to protect him in all his movements. At the seventh year, the king was brought out of hiding and crowned and anointed as the rightful king on David's throne. It was a happy day. The people clapped their hands and said, "Long live the king!" The wicked Athaliah was killed, and once again a light was kept burning on the throne of David.

It is a wonderful picture of one who was hidden and then manifested. This is the way it will be with regard to the Lord Jesus Christ.

"When Christ who is our life appears, then you also will appear with Him in glory" (verse 4).

The world does not see the glory of the Lord today; we see Him by faith! Those around us do not know of our life with Christ, but they will know in the day of manifestation. This is not His coming *for* us at the Rapture but our coming *with* Him at His appearing. It should be noted that when the *appearing* of Christ is the subject, it is connected with our *practical living*. This is borne out in the next sections.

COLOSSIANS 3:5-7 — PUT TO DEATH

This section is very practical in its content. There is to be a ruthless dealing with ourselves. We would think of it as self-discipline. Let's look first at verse 5:

"Therefore put to death your members which are on the earth: fornication, uncleanness, passion, evil desire, and covetousness, which is idolatry."

As we have been taught in the previous section that we are dead to our old life in Christ, then there is to be a corresponding change of behaviour. So the vital word is, "put to death".

We may never have been guilty of the awful features outlined in our verse but we have a nature capable of them all. The Apostle uses the expression "your members". We might gain the impression, just reading the verse, that the members are the ugly features themselves.

Looking at Paul's other letters, however, the impression is that they refer to the members of our body through which these things show themselves. To make this a little clearer, just consider a brief passage from Paul's letter to the Romans:

> "...For just as you presented your members as slaves of uncleanness, ... so now present your members as slaves of righteousness for holiness" (Romans 6:19).

You may recall some words of the Lord Jesus, when He was on earth and speaking to His disciples, He said,

> "If your hand or foot causes you to sin, cut it off and cast it from you. ... And if your eye causes you to sin, pluck it out and cast it from you" (Matthew 18:8-9).

No one would think that the Lord Jesus was referring to any physical mutilation; of course not! He was speaking of the need for self-judgement *very* similar to the sentiments of Colossians 3.

Let's have another illustration from the Old Testament scriptures, this time from the book of Joshua. After forty years wandering in the wilderness, Israel had crossed the river Jordan. Joshua was instructed to take out of the midst of the river Jordan twelve stones, each one representing a tribe of Israel. They were to be a memorial reminding them of their deliverance into the Promised Land. They were to set up a cairn of stones in the place where they lodged that night. Eventually they were set up again in a place called Gilgal (Joshua 4). As we today look back on these stones taken out of the waters of death by the Holy Spirit, we can see the truth we have considered in Colossians 3: Raised with Christ!!

Gilgal was the scene of another event of great importance. The generation which crossed Jordan was different from that which left Egypt. None of this company had been circumcised. This was an important rite for Israel as God had given it to His people many years previously as a mark of the relationship that was between them. It involved all the males among them and was to be done when each was eight days old.

In Joshua 5:2 we read,

> "At that time the LORD said to Joshua, 'Make flint knives for yourself, and circumcise the sons of Israel again the second time.'"

This does not apply to the Christian in any physical way; it is referred to in Colossians 2:11 and is related to the cross of Christ.

> "In Him you were also circumcised with the circumcision made *without hands*, by putting off the body of the sins of the flesh, by the circumcision of Christ".

The flesh is that principle of sin which is in each of us and is incapable of any good. It was judged [*cut off*] in the death of our Lord Jesus. The believer accepts this as true. Believers assent to this in baptism.

46

In these verses in Colossians 3, however, it is practical. We must "put to death" our "members which are on the earth". Gilgal, as a type for us, tells of the need of rigorous self-judgement. Gilgal became a base of operations in the land of Canaan. Whenever a conquest was made and battles were won, the Israelites were to return to the base again. There is a lesson for us here. When we imagine that we are making progress in our lives as Christians, let us be vigilant against the subtle foe within. Let us be thankful that, as well as having a new life in Christ, there is the indwelling Spirit to be our help.

Before leaving this section of our chapter, just consider verse 6, referring to the awful features outlined in verse 5:

"Because of these things the wrath of God is coming upon the sons of disobedience".

This is very solemn; God does not pass over sin lightly. He has provided salvation for us freely through the Lord Jesus. The cost was great: His precious blood. This salvation may be ours through faith in Him.

COLOSSIANS 3:8-17 — A CHANGE OF CLOTHES

We move on a little further, in this wonderful chapter. It is still very practical. The subject to be considered in this section is 'the old man and the new man'. The exhortations are a little different from those we have already looked at. Instead of 'putting to death', it becomes a matter of 'putting off' and 'putting on'. The impression is given of a change of clothes. We will keep this picture in mind. The question is, of course, What is "the old man"? The Apostle does not say! He just leaves it in the abstract. Can we get some light elsewhere? In Romans 6:6 we get some help, because the writer puts the truth right on to our doorstep, not now in the abstract:

"knowing this, that *our* old man was crucified with Him, that the body of sin might be done away with, that we should no longer be slaves of sin."

How important is the cross! Let us never underestimate its value! The old man, then, is that old nature we all inherited from Adam and it was crucified with Christ at Calvary. We need to accept these statements by faith and act upon them.

Let's read verses 8-9 of Colossians 3:

"But now you yourselves are to put off all these: anger, wrath, malice, blasphemy, filthy language out of your mouth. Do not lie to one another, since you *have* put off the old man with his deeds".

The features given here are not quite the same as those given in verse 5, but some of them may easily come into evidence and spoil Christian fellowship. How easy it is to give way to anger, wrath and even malice when things don't go our way! We must put them off and be finished with them. But the verse goes on to say that *we have* put off the old man.

How do we understand this? Think again of Romans 6:6, where we learned that "our old man was crucified with Him". This provides the answer to our question. It is in the light of the cross of Christ that verse 9 of our chapter says, "you *have* put off the old man". But if it is true in fact, we must deal with the old man in practice. We will move on now. Let's look at verse 10:

"and *have* put on the new man who is renewed in knowledge according to the image of Him who created him".

We had no part in this; it was God's sovereign work in our heart.

The new man is said here, and also in Ephesians 4:24, to be "created". In an earlier letter of the Apostle Paul there is a passage that goes like this,

"So if any one [be] in Christ, [there is] a new creation" (2 Corinthians 5:17, N.Tr.).

Because these things are true of us, we are to put on new clothes. This is practical! It is important to point out that the new man is not the Lord Jesus personally, but the characteristics of the new man were seen in Him.

Let's consider verse 12:

"Therefore, as the elect of God, holy and beloved, put on tender mercies, kindness, humility, meekness, longsuffering".

How often, as believers, we have thought about the life of the Lord Jesus. Every feature given here was seen in Him. The sense here is that we have determined to do this once for all and then seek the help of the Lord to go on. It is also true that we are to be Christ-like in our daily walk. What an effect these expressions of Christ should have on our fellowship with one another!

Let's think of one more illustration from the Old Testament, this time in 2 Kings 2. We read there of two prophets, Elijah and Elisha. They were evil days; God's people had turned to the worship of Baal, and Elijah had been called to restore them to the worship of Jehovah. Elijah had been told that when his work was done he would be taken up to heaven in a whirlwind and Elisha was to take his place.

As this time drew near, they made an interesting journey together. They visited certain places of significance until they reached the river Jordan. We are told that Elijah took his cloak and wrapped it together and smote the waters and they parted and they both crossed over. If Elisha was to take Elijah's place in power, everything depended on seeing him taken up. It did happen as God had said. Elijah was taken up in a whirlwind and Elisha witnessed it and then saw him no more. The reaction of Elisha was that he took hold of his own clothes and rent them in two pieces. He took up the cloak that fell off Elijah and went back and stood by the bank of Jordan. With the cloak, he parted the waters again and went over. There were some who saw it all happen and they said, "The spirit of Elijah rests on Elisha." There had been a change of clothes! We are reminded here of what was said of Peter and John in Acts 4:13,

"They realized that they had been with Jesus."

This incident takes us back to our first point in this chapter. We are to look above to where Christ is and thus gain the necessary power to be Christ-like in our lives. Others looking on will see the change.

THE OVERCOAT

Verse 14 says,

"But above all these things put on love, which is the bond of perfection."

All will be bonded together by love; without it there will be little power.

The consideration of 'the old man and the new man' in this section of our chapter ends with a reference to *"the peace of Christ"* (verse 15, N.Tr.) to enable us to be true to the truth of the one body in our relationships with other believers. *"The word of Christ"* (verse 16) is to dwell in us to give us the instruction we need and that spiritual joy that would have us singing with grace in our hearts to the

Lord. Our final verse summarises the scope of the practical Christ-like life:

"And *whatever* you do in word or deed, do *all* in the name of the Lord Jesus, giving thanks to God the Father through Him" (verse 17).

May the Lord help us that, in all the circumstances of our lives, it may be true that in reality Christ *"is our life"* (3:4).

Colossians 3:18–4:1
You serve the Lord Christ

BY GORDON KELL

Elizabeth Fry, who worked so hard to improve conditions in Victorian prisons, once said, "Since my heart was touched at seventeen, I believe I have never awakened from sleep, in sickness or in health, by day or by night, without my first waking thought being how best I might serve my Lord." The Apostle Paul, in 1 Thessalonians 1:9, reminds his readers that they had "turned to God from idols to serve the living and true God." In the first century of Christianity idolatry was widespread. It did not simply mean having a shrine to an idol in the corner of a room in your house or going one day a week to a temple to worship a false God. No, idolatry affected everything: personal life, family life, food, business, etc. Every aspect of community life was governed by idolatry. When the Thessalonians believed the Gospel they stopped serving idols and began to serve God. Just as the whole of their lives had been governed by idolatry, now they committed the whole of their lives to God's service. In the words of Romans 12:1, they presented their lives as living sacrifices.

RELATIONSHIPS

In our passage, Paul explains in more detail what it means to "serve the Lord Christ." He does this by teaching us about service within a framework of relationships. The relationships he highlights are:

- wives and husbands;

- fathers and children;

- employees and employers.

When we think about Christian service it is often in relation to some Christian activity such as preaching or teaching, working with young people, etc. But Christian service is also carried out in the everyday circumstances and relationships of life. Do we think of our marriages, our responsibilities as parents, our jobs, as opportunities to serve the Lord Jesus? This is our challenge.

COLOSSIANS 3:18-19 — WIVES AND HUSBANDS

WIVES

The first act of service presented to us is that of wives. I suppose if we had been writing Colossians we might have started with husbands. But Paul, both here and in similar verses in Ephesians 5, puts the wives first. When it comes to the success and stability of the Christian home the role of the wife is vital. For too long the role of women as wives, mothers and home makers has been belittled. The struggle for women's independence became paramount. Now there are signs, both in the USA and Europe, that some people are beginning to realise the importance of the woman's role in the home, in terms of stable family life and the way this underpins society. Paul's teaching about the role of women has often been criticised. It has even been suggested that it was based upon his dislike of them. However, an intelligent reader of his writings would soon discover the tremendous affection and admiration he had for the many women he knew and had worked with. No, Paul explains in his writings God's pattern for the relationships men and women enjoy and responsibilities they have. The relationship of a wife to her husband is characterised by submission. This statement taken in isolation would seem unfair. But it has to be understood within the context of Christian marriage in which Paul commands the husbands to,

> "love your wives, just as Christ also loved the Church and gave Himself for her" (Ephesians 5:25).

The use of the word "submission" in the Bible is often mis-interpreted as weakness and as only applying to women. But when we look more carefully at the Bible teaching about submission we find this is not true. In 1 Peter 5:5 we read,

> "Likewise you younger people, submit yourselves to your elders. Yes, all of you be submissive to one another, and be clothed with humility".

In others words, all Christians are to be marked by a willingness to honour one another and always to act with humility. Peter uses the expression "be clothed with humility". This could be a reference to his experience of the humility of the Lord Jesus in John 13. In that chapter the Lord Jesus washes the disciples' feet. This was the act of a common household servant, probably a slave. It says there in verse 4 that Jesus "laid aside His garments, took a towel and girded Himself." The greatest exponent of submission and humility was the Lord Jesus. These are the characteristics of the Great Servant. If we want to be effective in our service we have to learn submission to God's word and humility in obeying it.

HUSBANDS

The submission of a wife to her husband is described in verse 19 as "fitting in the Lord." The word "fitting" means "to have come up to". In expressing such submission the wife is demonstrating the character of the Lord Jesus in her marriage. Husbands, on the other hand, are reminded to love their wives. It is remarkable that, in the Bible, wives are only once asked to love their husbands. This occurs in Titus 2:4 and refers to young wives. On the other hand, on several occasions husbands are reminded to love their wives; for example, in Ephesians 5:

> "So husbands ought to love their own wives as their own bodies; ..." (verse 28).

> "Nevertheless let each one of you in particular so love his own wife as himself, ..." (verse 33).

It seems to me that women have a greater ability to demonstrate love whereas men are apt to fail in showing affection. Paul *commands* husbands to show love to their wives. The background to this teaching is important. Paul lived at a time when women, like slaves, were treated as the property of their husbands. He does not exhort men to demonstrate *authority* but *love*. It was common for men to be angry and even violent towards their wives, as today, and not to be held accountable for cruel actions. Paul insists that this is not the behaviour of a Christian, who is always to act in love and gentleness towards his wife.

Within marriage there is the service of love. In Galatians 5:13 Paul writes, "through love serve one another." This service of love is seen in a most beautiful way within a Christian marriage. We live in an age where women are still abused within and outside of marriage – an age in which men's actions are too often characterised by violence. The happiness of a true Christian marriage serves to show to the world the love of Christ in the behaviour of the wife and husband.

COLOSSIANS 3:20-21 — CHILDREN AND FATHERS

CHILDREN

Today we hear a lot today about civil disobedience and the growing resentment towards authority. More than ever, the disruptiveness of children and the problems of discipline at home and in school are in the news. These are not new problems. Paul was obviously aware of the difficulty of disobedient children in his own day. And it is very interesting that in verse 20 he speaks directly to children. As with adults, the example he always presents is the Lord Jesus. Jewish children had been brought up with an understanding of the Law. In it they were commanded to —

> "Honour your father and you mother, that your days be long upon the land which the LORD your God is giving you" (Exodus 20:12).

It is striking that Luke reminds us of the childhood of the Lord Jesus. When He was twelve years old we read that,

> "He went down with them [that is, His parents] and came to Nazareth, and was subject to them" (Luke 2:51).

Most children get to a stage where they think they know more than their parents. When Jesus was a child He *did* know more than His parents. But He still obeyed them. It is amazing to think that the very Person who sustains the whole of creation entered not only into that creation but into the very relationships we know as parents and children. The Lord Jesus always valued human relationships and the responsibilities they brought. At the beginning of His life He demonstrated obedience towards

His parents. At the end of His life, as He died on the cross, He ensured that His mother would be properly cared for by asking John to look after her. The Lord Jesus' service included obedience to His earthly parents and responsibility for them. There is little wonder that He is pleased when Christian children follow His example.

FATHERS

But there is another side to this story. If children are to be obedient, fathers are not to discourage them (verse 21). It is once again interesting that Paul did not see mothers as a discouragement to children. In fact, in 2 Timothy 1:5, he remembers the great *encouragement* Timothy's mother and grandmother were to his young friend, and how he had been taught the Scriptures from childhood.

Paul did find it necessary to warn fathers not to discourage their children. The problem highlighted by Paul was the tendency always to find fault with children or perhaps just some of them. The result, and it can cause lifelong damage, is that the child feels it can do no right and becomes despondent. There is today the added danger that parents can become so ambitious for their children, even to the extent of trying to fulfil their own ambitions through their children. When children do not meet their parents' expectations, they are criticised and sometimes persecuted for their failures. We have to recognise that our children are individuals.

It is for Christian parents to provide the protection, authority and discipline that they need. We are encouraged to —

"bring them up in the training and admonition of the Lord" (Ephesians 6:4).

The word for "training" applies to teaching by example and action. This is complemented by "admonition", which emphasizes training by what we say. A Christian parent has to be consistent in word and action; and this is the service which fathers, in particular, are encouraged to undertake. An effective father is neither a bully nor a weak-willed man who gives way to the will of his children. A father is a man who serves the Lord by gently leading and keeping his children in the right direction in life. I remember reading that D. L. Moody, the remarkable American evangelist, made it a rule to apologise to his children when he got it wrong. Openness and honesty with our children will always enhance their respect for adults. Stubbornness and unfairness will always diminish that respect.

COLOSSIANS 3:22–4:1 — EMPLOYEES AND EMPLOYERS

From verse 22 Paul addresses employees and employers. Of course, in his day, many employees were slaves. In his letter to his friend Philemon, Paul deals with the matter of a runaway slave called Onesimus. It was very important to the Christian testimony that Christian masters and Christian servants lived out their faith in Christ. One of the great dangers was that Christian masters might continue to treat their servants unjustly and with little respect. The other danger was that Christian servants, who now knew liberty in Christ, might show disrespect towards their masters and bring the Gospel into disrepute. Paul's teaching about these relationships demonstrated how true Christians could be a real witness in the way they fulfilled their responsibilities at work. As most of us spend a good deal of time working for a living, this passage has a lot to say to us today.

EMPLOYEES

Verses 22 and 23 show us that the true Christian regards everyday work as a service to Christ. Work has always had the same problems. Some people do as little work as possible because they are lazy or do not think they are paid enough. Some work hard only when they are being watched and try to curry favour with their bosses. Some complain endlessly about the conditions of work or are very unhappy about their bosses. Often there are genuine reasons for complaints and such things need to be addressed. But Paul is encouraging Christians to do everything in the light of serving a greater Master – the Lord. We have a Lord in heaven to whom we shall one day give an account of our service. He will not want to hear excuses like "I didn't have a good boss", or "My work wasn't very interesting". He will ask how we served Him in the circumstances He placed us.

I heard recently heard of a family where the son never did any housework. This used to really annoy his sister. The son started university and after his first year came back home. As soon as the family finished their meal, he began clearing the dishes and then started the washing up. His sister could not believe the change she was seeing. When she asked him about his new behaviour, he told her how he had been taken along to the Christian Union at university and had been become a Christian. It was not long before the sister took the same step of faith and now the whole family are believers. Why? Because a new Christian had the right attitude to work. Nothing is too menial to be a witness to the Saviour.

Paul encourages the Colossian servants to undertake their service as something which is done for Christ and in a Christ-like spirit. If all Christians worked like this, what a difference our testimony would make. The New International Version translates verse 23,

"Whatever you do, work at it with all your heart, as working for the Lord, not for human masters" (NIV).

This verse should transform our view of everyday work because not only does it mean we are working *for* the Lord but that the work itself is valued *by* the Lord. The Gospels remind us that the Lord Jesus values even a cup of water given to one in need. This is why Paul goes on to speak in the next verse of reward. This is a very touching verse. A slave was not paid for his work. He was owned and had no real possessions because everything belonged to his master. When Paul writes, "knowing that from the Lord you will receive the reward of the inheritance", he was not simply thinking of the future. He is saying that the Lord Himself is the present possession of His people. The Christian experience of knowing joy and power in the most adverse circumstances comes from Christ reigning in our hearts and lives *now*. In the future we shall enter into all the fullness of the life which we really have in Christ.

But Paul also reminds us that wrong-doing, whether by master or slave, will be the subject of God's judgement. This judgement has no regard to status or wealth. God will judge perfectly. This is in stark contrast to the many injustices we witness in the world.

Today we also face other difficulties at work. One is the tremendous pressure and stress which work places upon the individual and the family. It is very important that work does not undermine relationships and family life. This can happen because the demands of work are too great to bear. It can also happen because we become so absorbed in our work that we no longer have time for the vital relationships in our lives. We have to ask ourselves the reasons why these things happen. Have we become covetous? Are we striving too competitively in our work? Are we serving ourselves rather than the Lord and those we love? It is important to sit down especially with our spouses to evaluate the direction our work is taking us. We need to prioritise things in our lives so that the work we do to live, does not become life itself. Many solid marriages have failed because ambition and the pressure of work have become too great. It is equally important that, in serving the Lord, we do not overlook the service He has given us in regard to our families. Albert Einstein was wise when he wrote that we should, "Try not to become a man of success but rather try to become a man of value."

To help us to do this it is sometimes a good thing to sit down and list all the commitments we have. Then look at each one and ask ourselves the question, "Is this something the Lord wants me to do?"

A few years ago at a young couple's weekend my wife and I organised, a couple were complaining about all the work they had to do. It was obvious everything had become too much for them. We asked them why they did certain things and it became clear they had gradually taken on so much work that they could not carry on. We suggested they looked at all these responsibilities carefully and asked themselves which ones the Lord really expected them to do and which ones were over-commitments. The next year they came to the weekend and told us that they had reviewed their commitments and reduced them. As a consequence, they were a much happier family. William Gurnall wrote, "God will not thank thee for doing that which He did not set thee about" (*The Christian in Complete Armour*, 1669). It is good advice.

EMPLOYERS

In Colossians 4:1, Paul turns to Christian employers. He reminds them that they also have a Master who is in heaven. They were responsible to treat their servants with justice and fairness. The world has always suffered from injustice and unfairness. The greatest example of this was when the Lord Jesus was judged and crucified. Justice and fairness are attributes of God Himself and as His people we are expected to demonstrate these same features. Paul emphasizes the special responsibility which Christian employers have in regard to these qualities.

The history of industrial relations in the United Kingdom is one which is born out of the conflicts between employees and employers. A lot of this history involves the exploitation of workers who for many centuries suffered long hours, very arduous work, and lived in extreme poverty. Throughout the world today, there is still much evidence of the same injustices. Christian employers should never be associated with such practices.

The standard Paul sets before Christians, with such responsibilities, is that they are to be just and fair. And this was to be done in a spirit of goodwill. It is possible coldly to administer justice, rather like judges with no particular empathy with the person receiving the justice.

We have a fine example of an employer with good employee relationships in the book of Ruth in the Old Testament. It is Boaz, Ruth's future husband, and the great grandfather of King David. We are introduced to him in the second chapter. He was an wealthy employer with a big workforce. It is evident that he had a remarkable relationship with the people he employed. It was one of mutual respect. His sense of justice and fairness is seen in the way he treats Ruth who was the lowliest of his employees. But he also is remarkable in another way. He worked with his employees. He worked in the fields with them and he even ate meals and slept in the same building with his workers during the harvest time. In other words, he was close to those he was responsible for and knew and treated them well. People who take on the role of employer or boss often allow these positions to make them distant and detached from those who work for them. Boaz led by example. He was not afraid to do the same work or to spend time with those who worked for him. In so doing he gained the respect and affection of his employees. We have a Lord and Master in heaven who was never afraid to do the work of a slave and worked alongside His disciples for three years to train them in true service. Equally, the Saviour in heaven now supports us in our service for Him. He is a just and fair Master. And Christian employers are in a unique position to demonstrate the features of Christ as they serve Him in this capacity.

This great subject of service in our everyday lives is so important to the witness we have in today's world. The service towards each other in the vital relationships of wives and husbands, parents and children, and employees and employers, demonstrates true Christianity in a world where such relationships are breaking down. Let us not be afraid of being obedient to God's word but prove the greatness of His ability to bless us in these areas of our lives. This is summed by some words I read recently, "When all that *you are* is available to all that *God is*, then all that *God is* is available to all that *you are*" (Major Ian Thomas, *The Indwelling Life of Christ*).

Colossians 4:2-18
Pray, walk and talk

BY DAVID ANDERSON

My wife child-minds Jack, who is 10 months old. For the past two or three months now, he has been trying to get to his feet to walk. He has found his baby-walker extremely useful in this respect, but he is best at sideways walking, along furniture and the like. But at the same time he has been frustrated in the sitting position, because he has been unable to crawl. We kept on telling him that "you have got to learn to crawl before you can walk". Eventually the penny dropped, and he now moves around the floor in a manner resembling a slug!

We have titled this passage 'Pray, Walk and Talk'. In it Paul was not advising the Christians at Colossae that prayer precedes walk and talk. Rather it is that prayer, walk and talk are all necessary component parts of practical Christian life – they are on-going, cyclic activities.

Baby Jack is at the normal stage of development for a boy of his age. As you would expect, his five-year-old sister, Emily, has no problems talking! (and she's quite a good walker). Luke, their older brother, is somewhat more advanced than either of them. They each will, in the course of time, grow up into adulthood, but they all will continue to be involved in these activities of life, walking and talking.

Paul has been pressing similar ideas of Christian growth into maturity in this letter to the Colossians. In 1:9-10 he prays for them —

"...that you may be filled with the knowledge of His will in all wisdom and spiritual understanding; that you may walk worthy of the Lord, fully pleasing Him, being fruitful in every good work and increasing in the knowledge of God".

Then in 2:6-7 —

"As you therefore have received Christ Jesus the Lord, so walk in Him, rooted and built up in Him and established in the faith, as you have been taught, abounding in it with thanksgiving."

Here in 4:2 he says,

"Continue earnestly in prayer...",

which introduces our first watchword: *pray*.

COLOSSIANS 4:2-4 — PRAY

Now we know that Jack, Emily, and Luke will not continue to develop in life without constant attention to their well-being from their parents and from others, such as my wife. Similarly, without constant attention to prayer, the Christian will not be able either to develop or maintain those necessary characteristics of Christ – the "new man", as it is described in 3:10. These characteristics are vital for Christian witness, contrasting as they do with the old style of life lived before conversion. The verses following on from 3:10, through to 4:1, remind us that these features are primarily seen in our church fellowships, our families, and in our secular work. And prior to 3:10, Paul has already stressed the necessity of personal piety. No wonder then that he now urges "continue earnestly in prayer". Prayer must form an integral part of the Christian's life in order for walk and talk to be kept in line with the exhortation from 3:17,

> "And whatever you do in word or deed, do all in the name of the Lord Jesus, giving thanks to God the Father through Him."

ENDURANCE IN PRAYER

First of all, then, endurance in prayer is vital. I remember when one of my former Sunday School scholars was trying to assure me that he had not given up the Faith, that I asked him about his personal communion with the Lord. He had to admit that he no longer had a prayer life. A constant New Testament theme about the Christian faith is continuance, especially in prayer. For example: in Acts 2:42, where it is seen as one of the four pillars of church life —

> "...they *continued steadfastly* in the apostles' doctrine and fellowship, in the breaking of bread, and in prayers";

in Romans 12:12 —

> "...*continuing steadfastly* in prayer";

and in the very first of Paul's letters, to a young church, the Thessalonians, he urges in 1 Thessalonians 5:17,

> "pray *without ceasing*".

THE STRUGGLE OF PRAYER

Secondly, verse 2 indicates that prayer will always be a struggle, a battle that is constantly to be fought. Why? – Because the Enemy, the Devil, is continually trying to break through and break down any effective witness to Christ, particularly that demonstrated in practical Christian living.

VIGILANCE IN PRAYER

Hence the need to be "vigilant in [prayer]". We are to be on our guard, on the look-out as to things in the world, happenings in society and in government, things affecting our families and churches, so that we are awake to every situation, and not taken by surprise by any event. On the contrary we should anticipate it by prayer with thanksgiving. As verse 2 says,

"Continue earnestly in prayer, being vigilant in it with thanksgiving".

THANKSGIVING

On the one hand, then, a state of spiritual alertness is required; on the other hand, our gratitude to God for every victory gained, and every provision of His grace, is also to be expressed. Thanksgiving is an aspect of prayer that can so easily be forgotten. But we can see from Paul's mention of it in this letter the importance which he gave to it. The references are:

- We *give thanks* to the God and Father of our Lord Jesus Christ, praying always for you (1:3)

- ...*giving thanks* to the Father who has qualified us to be partakers of the inheritance of the saints in the light (1:12)

- …rooted and built up in Him and established in the faith, as you have been taught, abounding in it *with thanksgiving* (2:7)

- And let the peace of God rule in your hearts, to which also you were called in one body; and *be thankful* (3:15)

- And whatever you do in word or deed, do all in the name of the Lord Jesus, *giving thanks* to God the Father through Him (3:17)

- Continue earnestly in prayer, being vigilant in it *with thanksgiving* (4:2)

And we are to remember that he wrote this instruction from a prison cell!

PRAYING FOR OTHERS

But prayer is not only to be made for ourselves, it is for others also. Paul enjoins the Colossians in verses 3-4 —

> "meanwhile praying also for us, that God would open to us a door for the word, to speak the mystery of Christ, for which I am also in chains, that I may make it manifest, as I ought to speak."

He knew that his own desire, stated in 1:28 —

> "…that we may present every man perfect in Christ Jesus",

was insufficient without God's help. He wanted to be sure that, although he willingly laboured in this special stewardship, that this striving would be by God working mightily in him. The prayers of the Christians at Colossae were necessary in this respect. They were also to pray that Paul would fill out his ministry by fully preaching the truth about Christ, here called "the mystery of Christ".

According to his explanation of his duties in 1:24-29, this meant that he had to explain in full the revelation of God. It was about the riches of the glory of this secret of the exalted Christ, not just the fundamentals of the Gospel of His grace. So aware was he of this great commission that he never presumed, but always asked believers to pray: "that I may make it manifest, as I ought to speak."

Paul was also aware of the Enemy's action in trying to prevent the doors of the Gospel being opened. He refers in verse 3 to the fact that his imprisonment was on account of this mystery, "for which I am also in chains." It has always seemed strange to me that men should shut up in prison the messenger carrying the best things from God, "all the treasures of wisdom and knowledge" (2:3). But I realise that it is the Devil's activity behind the scenes.

When we pray for the Lord's servants who are spreading the Word of God, it should also be along these lines. In this respect it is useful to have up-to-date information on their activities, with the accompanying successes and frustrations, such as we get in missionary prayer letters and lists. This information is somewhat easier to obtain in today's world of advanced communications, than it was here with Paul who had to send Tychicus with the news.

Watch and *pray* are good watchwords with which to conclude this consideration on prayer.

COLOSSIANS 4:5 — WALK

Next Paul exhorts the Colossians in verse 5 to —

> "Walk in wisdom toward those who are outside, redeeming the time."

This brings us to discuss our second watchword: *walk*. It is frequently used in the New Testament to describe the whole conduct of daily Christian life. Believers must be careful about the way they live. They must not convey a bad impression of the Gospel because life is mainly lived out before unbelievers, or outsiders, as they are called here in verse 5.

The same kind of watchfulness that we saw was necessary for prayer is again called for in our walk. We have to "redeem the time", that is to look out for, seize, and make good the opportunities for witnessing which come along day by day, not letting any of them slip by. Such opportunities no doubt equate to the "open door for the word" of verse 3. They are the possibilities of what God might do in or through us to present the claims of Christ to others. For example, I know a man who was constantly provoked by his workmates for his faith in Christ. An opportunity came one day, during an overtime late-shift, to respond directly to one of the most aggressive young men. That young man was soon convicted of his sins, and knelt down on the shop-floor in repentance towards God and faith toward our Lord Jesus Christ!

COLOSSIANS 4:6 — TALK

Witness to Christ will definitely involve *talk*, our third watchword. As verse 6 states:

> "Let your speech always be with grace, seasoned with salt, that you may know how you ought to answer each one."

Our speech is never to be cheap or coarse, rather, it must always bear upon it the stamp of the Gospel, that is, grace. It should be appropriate as regards the time, the place and the person, and should not compromise truth – it needs to be "seasoned with salt". Hence the general tone of our everyday communications, as well as what is said, must commend the Gospel so that people will ask about the hope that is in us. Let us be like the Master, who was "full of grace and truth" (John 1:14). He always said the right things in the right manner, able to discern the need for grace, or salt, or both.

COLOSSIANS 4:7-18 — EXAMPLES

A casual reading of the rest of the chapter may suggest that we have finished with our watchwords. However we find rather the reverse is true. The different people mentioned here are living out practically both the meaning of these watchwords and the rest of the teaching of the letter. In these verses *service* is prominent now, just as *witness* was in the previous verses.

TYCHICUS

A lovely description of Tychicus is given in verse 7: a beloved brother, a faithful minister, a fellow servant. These show how he *walked* as a Christian. His task was to deliver the letter from Paul to the Colossians. Accompanying him was Onesimus, and together they were to bring the news about Paul. Not only could Tychicus' 'talk' be relied upon in this respect, but such was his 'walk' that he was given pastoral duties as well. In verse 8 Paul tells them —

> "I am sending him to you for this very purpose, that he may know your circumstances and comfort your hearts."

Tychicus was competent to assess their needs and to minister the Word to them.

ONESIMUS

Before leaving verse 9, we can see in Onesimus an example of the meaning of 1:13 —

71

"[The Father] has delivered us from the power of darkness and conveyed us into the kingdom of the Son of His love".

Onesimus had been converted to Christ after running away from Philemon, his master, then meeting up with Paul in prison. Sin may have caused this slave to steal and run away, but God, as it were, picked him up and placed him down under the Lordship of Christ. His literal return from another country to his native country and to his master, would add to the understanding of the Colossians concerning this spiritual truth. It would also underline to them that they were all enslaved to Christ.

MARK, LUKE, DEMAS AND OTHERS

It is good when the Lord's servants can team up together as Tychicus and Onesimus did. Aristarchus could not join them because he was a prisoner, like Paul. However, along with his fellow Jews, Mark and Jesus, called Justus, he could send his greetings. Not that the latter were not free to go, rather they were committed to stay to help Paul. Mark did have some plans to visit Colossae, but these three servants had their eyes set on the future glory, they were working for the kingdom of God. So, in all of their movements, and for the timing of such, they subjected themselves to the will of God for their lives.

Verse 14 adds Luke and Demas, Gentiles, to the greetings, which are sent also to "the brethren who are in Laodicea" and to Nymphas and "the church that is in his house" (verse 15). From the greetings list we see consistent conduct in "the beloved physician", failure but full recovery in Mark (see Acts 15:37-38, 2 Timothy 4:11), and a turning back into the world by Demas (2 Timothy 4:10). This raises the challenge with us: how committed are we to the service of God? And are we like Paul? –

appreciative of the help of a Luke, willing to forget the shortcomings of a Mark, and ready to grieve when a Demas lets us down.

<small>EPAPHRAS</small>

Verse 12 turns from the walking and talking of Paul's companions and messengers, to the prayers of Epaphras, who is described as "our dear fellow servant, who is a faithful minister of Christ on your behalf" in 1:7. We are told in that same verse that he had brought the Gospel to Colossae and the surrounding districts, establishing churches there in the Lycus river valley. This is perhaps why he wanted them to fully grasp Paul's teaching and for it to become fully effective in their lives, "that you may stand perfect and complete in all the will of God."

Here we can identify some of the key words of this letter again. They are: *perfect, complete, all*, and *will.*

The idea of being *perfect* is to be mature, fully grown, as we have mentioned from Paul's goal in 1:28 – "every man perfect in Christ Jesus." The thought of being *complete* occurs several times in the letter. They are:

- "filled" (or filled full) in 1:9;

- "the fullness" in 1:19 and 2:9;

- "fulfil" in 1:25 and later in 4:17;

- "full assurance" in 2:2;

- "complete" in 2:10 as well as here in 4:12.

The fullness dwells in Christ, and we are complete in Him. God wants this enrichment to come out in our lives.

In 1:9 Paul himself had prayed for these believers in a general way that they would grasp the *Will* of God. This

Will can be summarised using words from chapter 1. They are in verse 18:

"that in all things He [that is, Christ] may have the pre-eminence";

and in verse 27:

"...Christ in you, the hope of glory."

Epaphras' intimate knowledge of his converts enabled him to pray in a specific way, that they would be in *all* the will of God. He knew their circumstances, the stage that they had reached in Christian development, the realm of their service, and he would be aware of the dangers of their being side-tracked by false teaching.

To illustrate, using baby Jack again, his parents wish to see him grow through all stages of babyhood and boyhood into a mature adult, who will fill out his place in society and realise his full potential. Crawling like a slug is only satisfactory for another month or so, when he can walk properly, and progress from there. They will be active in assisting him in every way, anxious to protect him from every danger, and careful to monitor his development. Similarly, Epaphras, a true spiritual father, was not content with anything less than the full knowledge of God's will and its full expression in the lives of these Lycus valley believers.

Notice again the persistent effort that is a feature of prayer. "Always labouring fervently" means he overcame all difficulties, and with great zeal, gave himself totally to it. Epaphras had learnt how to pray in this intense way by praying with Paul. 2:1 tells of Paul's great conflict for this group of churches. Epaphras joined Paul in that same fight for those at Colossae, at Hierapolis and at Laodicea, that they might understand these secrets about Christ, that they might be bound together in love, and live in all the will of God.

In order to learn the truth of God and then to practise His will we need the word of God. Hence, in verse 16, encouragement is given to these churches to use the Scriptures. They were enjoined publicly to read and to exchange the letters sent by the Apostles to each individual church, so as to be lacking in nothing. It has been well noted that if the Laodiceans had imbibed the teaching about Christ being everything from the Colossian letter, they would have not been accused later of self-sufficiency by the Lord Himself in Revelation 3:17. The prophetic nature of the letters to the churches in Revelation makes us realise how much we need these Colossian truths today.

ARCHIPPUS

The letter to Colossae ends on a very practical note with an individual, Archippus, singled out for special admonition.

> "And say to Archippus, 'Take heed to the ministry which you have received in the Lord, that you may fulfil it'" (verse 17).

Here we get that final use of the word *complete* or *fulfil*. We are not told the nature of his service, how much of it he was or was not doing, or whether he had been discouraged by something or someone. The point was that he had to get on and do it, emphasizing again that fully discharging the will of God is the only practical response that will satisfy God. We need to take this exhortation to ourselves today, so that in our prayer life, in our walk, and in our talk we may likewise fulfil what we have received from the Lord, especially from our study of this letter.

I end with two quotations from chapter 3:

"And whatever you do in word or deed, do all in the name of the Lord Jesus, giving thanks to God the Father through Him" (verse 17);

and:

"And whatever you do, do it heartily, as to the Lord..." (verse 23).

About the Authors

GEORGE STEVENS

George is a retired schoolteacher who lives in Ipswich. He became acquainted with the Lord from a young age attending a Baptist Sunday School and Young Sowers League. During his teenage years, he attended an Anglican church. He gained assurance of salvation in a Brethren assembly in Hounslow at about the age of twenty three. He has gone on to serve the Lord in a wide variety of ways including preaching and teaching.

DOUGLAS PETTMAN

Douglas has always been a resident of north London. He qualified as a chartered accountant and did National Service with the army. His business years were spent first within the profession. This was followed by directorships of several companies in this country and abroad. He is now retired. He is still involved in various aspects of church life, particularly in support of missionary work around the world and at home.

ERNIE BROWN

Ernie was born "between the wars" on Tyneside, which was then a major engineering production area. On leaving school, he received engineering training at a large engineering company there. On completion of his training, he served as a sea-going engineer with a major oil company for three years. The remaining years of his employment were spent with major energy supply companies in the North. Since retiring early from his secular employment, he has been engaged in Christian work in various parts of the UK, and occasionally abroad, as opportunity has arisen.

GEORGE BELL

George Bell (1922-2004) was originally from Tyneside. His job as a college lecturer in engineering led him to West Drayton and then to Birmingham. In his later years he settled in Ipswich with his family. He was much respected for his manner of life and as a Bible teacher both locally and nationally.

GORDON KELL

Gordon is much in demand as a Bible teacher, especially in dealing with practical subjects. He and his wife, June, a nurse, whom he married some 45 years ago, have long had an interest in helping and encouraging young Christians. They have one daughter and four grandchildren and live on the outskirts of Grimsby. He occasionally lectures at the New Tribes Mission and has broadcast on *Truth for Today* since its beginning.

DAVID ANDERSON

David lives in Newcastle on Tyne where he attends Edgefield Gospel Hall. He is married to Gillian and they have four adult children. David worked in the Active Pharmaceutical Ingredients sector of the chemical industry for 40 years as an analytical chemist, a quality manager and then as a company director before becoming a consultant. For many years, he was involved in organising children's summer camps at Fenham Farm, Northumberland. He is currently involved in preaching and teaching amongst Brethren assemblies and conferences. He also works as a tutor for UK and overseas students with Emmaus Bible School correspondence courses.

Other Books from Scripture Truth Publications

TRUTH FOR TODAY SERIES:

WHAT A GOD WE CHRISTIANS HAVE! BY GLENN BAXTER

ISBN 978-0-901860-59-0 (paperback)
208 pages; July 2011

WHO IS JESUS? BY COR BRUINS, DAVID PULMAN, PETER OLLERHEAD AND GEORGE BELL

ISBN 978-0-901860-57-6 (paperback)
60 pages; July 2011

SOME PROBLEMS CHRISTIANS FACE BY GORDON KELL, PETER OLLERHEAD AND JONATHAN HUGHES

ISBN 978-0-901860-58-3 (paperback)
68 pages; July 2011

UNDERSTANDING THE OLD TESTAMENT SERIES:

CHRIST IS MY BELOVED: A DEVOTIONAL STUDY OF PORTRAITS OF CHRIST IN THE SONG OF SOLOMON BY GEORGE E STEVENS

ISBN 978-0-901860-84-2 (paperback)
200 pages; October 2009

UNDERSTANDING THE NEW TESTAMENT SERIES:

THE EPISTLE TO THE COLOSSIANS: AN EXPOSITORY OUTLINE BY HAMILTON SMITH

ISBN 978-0-901860-90-3 (paperback)
68 pages; June 2009

UNDERSTANDING CHRISTIANITY SERIES:

REMEMBERING MY CREATOR SINCE MY YOUTH BY DAVID ANDERSON

ISBN 978-0-901860-93-4 (paperback)
192 pages; August 2014

Further Reading and Listening

READING

Full details of other books, magazines and calendars published by Scripture Truth Publications are available at our web site:

www.scripture-truth.org.uk

LISTENING

All programmes which have been broadcast on the *Truth for Today* radio programme at Premier Christian Radio are available for reading, printing or listening to again at:

www.truthfortoday.org.uk

We encourage you to make use of this resource.

www.ingramcontent.com/pod-product-compliance
Lightning Source LLC
Chambersburg PA
CBHW060036050426
42448CB00012B/3040